WALKS AROUND Richmond

10 WALKS 6 MILES OR LESS

Dalesman

Dalesman Publishing Company Ltd
Stable Courtyard, Broughton Hall,
Skipton, North Yorkshire BD23 3AZ

First Edition 1999

Text © Richard Musgrave

Illustrations © Christine Isherwood:
p5 Easby abbey, p8 ink cap fungi, p11 tawny owl, p13 jays,
p17 blackthorn and yew, p26 Grinton smelt mill, p29 primrose and
early purple orchid, p31 lapwings.

Maps by Jeremy Ashcroft

Cover: Richmond by Mike Kipling

A British Library Cataloguing in Publication record
is available for this book

ISBN 1 85568 157 9

Printed by Amadeus Press, Huddersfield

Contents

Introduction

Swaledale is a delightful place. There are lots of wonderful locations for the rambler to visit. This is made easier in the Richmond area, with a network of bus services emanating from the town centre. For bus service details contact 0345 124125. Two walks in this selection, 7 and 10, can't be reached by bus.

The ten walks I've devised cover the area between Richmond in the east and Reeth, ten miles west. Between these points, places like Marske, Marrick and Grinton are included. Ravensworth and Gilling West a little to the north of Richmond complete the starting locations.

Each of the walks should be suitable for reasonably fit families, eager to explore the countryside. Much enjoyment can be derived too — games like "stile spotting" can be a source of fun while developing powers of observation and initiative.

Regrettably at the time that these walks were made, waymarking, particularly around the Richmond area, wasn't good. The Coalsgarth Valley (walk 7) was almost devoid of signs. The rule I observed while researching that particular walk was to maintain a straight line, walking along the valley floor, keeping to the left of the beck at all times.

The absence of waymarking was disappointing. A simple sign can be so reassuring. However, don't be deterred. North Yorkshire County Council has indicated that matters should be improved by the time you read this book.

My sincere hope is that you enjoy the walks, and to further assist navigation all the walks are covered by O.S. map — Outdoor Leisure 30 (7-10) and Pathfinder 609 Richmond and Leyburn (1-6).

J. Richard Musgrave, January 1999

Richmond Falls & Easby Abbey

Length of walk: 3 miles. Start: Richmond obelisk
Terrain: Easy walking all the way

Perhaps one of the most popular rambles around the Richmond area, and rightly so. Only three miles in distance but packed with interest and wonderful scenery. Richmond Falls, Easby Abbey and St. Agatha's church

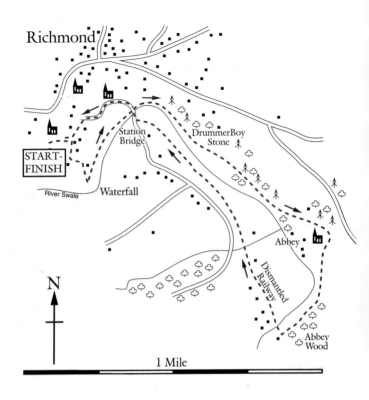

with its famous 13th century frescoes, all add to the enjoyment of this outing.

The obelisk in the centre of Richmond was erected in 1771, replacing a medieval market cross which had marked the site of Richmond's water supply. The well (or reservoir) is still beneath the obelisk. This is the start point.

Set off walking between the church and the Town Hall Hotel, descend the cobbled street, turning right at Barclays Bank to walk along Millgate.

Follow the road to a car park and Richmond Falls, then swing left to commence a brief riverside meander, walking along a tarred path.

When the path abruptly ends, veer left across the grass to another path. This leads to a wide gate to the left side of Station Bridge. Pass through the gate and cross the road to enter Lombards Wynd, turning right after a few paces.

The church of St. Mary's, to the left, contains choir stalls rescued from Easby Abbey, at the Dissolution.

Pass a house on the right then follow the wide path uphill into a woodland. There are good retrospective views hereabouts of the Swale and Richmond Castle. Pass the Drummer Boy stone (see plaque) and continue alongside the sports field, walking along a narrow track to arrive at a stile.

With the remains of the abbey in sight, head across the field to another stile resting beneath an imposing residence — St. Agatha's House, formerly the vicarage. Cross the stile then follow the track as it skirts around the church and the ruins — do visit both before continuing onwards. The church was built in 700AD, long before the monks arrived to build their abbey! The abbey was founded in 1152 by the Premonstratensian Order.

Leave the abbey and continue along the same track as before. Swing right close to Platelayers Cottage, to walk along the trackbed of the former Darlington-Richmond railway all the way to Richmond.

The railway station has been converted into a sports complex and swimming pool, but the row of cottages, which housed the railway staff, is still evident on the left as are the scant remains of St. Martin's Priory.

From the Station Bridge follow the road up into the town centre.

Billy Bank Wood & the River Swale

Length of walk: 3½ miles.
Start: Richmond-obelisk
Terrain: Two uphill sections, otherwise easy going.

Leave the obelisk walking past the Spar supermarket and the Talbot Hotel, following the road which tilts steeply downhill and is signposted "to the river".

Beyond a bend in the road notice the antique, wrought iron lamp standard on the left, and the information relating to Richmond's water supply and street illumination. At the bottom of the hill make towards the road bridge, looking right to see Culloden Tower, erected on the site of a castle, Hudswell Pele, to mark the victory at Culloden.

Cross the bridge (rebuilt between 1788-89) and turn immediately right, walking alongside the river. When the path divides keep following the main track as it rises into Billy Bank Wood

— surely a place to be at bluebell time. There is evidence of stone quarrying hereabouts.

Reaching an obvious junction swing right, descend to a footbridge, then swing right again walking down the steps to join the riverside path and turn left. Cross a stile, then follow the riverside path for almost a mile to reach a modern bridge across the river at a location known as Round Howe, a well-known beauty spot.

Cross the bridge, then proceed up the road facing to meet the main road. Cross over and turn left. Walk the road for 50 yards then turn into an uneven lane on the right. Hudswell Woods lie across the river to the left — a beautiful sight in autumn.

A short distance before reaching a large barn turn right and begin a long

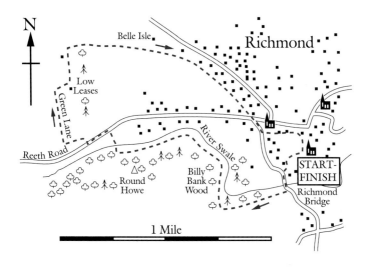

ascent, using a lane known as Green Lane. It is colourful in season and offers a splendid view, on the right, of Richmond Castle.

Go past Low Leases, a home with a superlative outlook, then continue along the access road which eventually merges with a road. Turn right here, and follow the road back into Richmond, passing some fine allotments along the way.

At the road junction keep left, then soon afterwards cross the busy road to enter Cravengate — look for the Angling Centre. Turn left into the cobbled Newbiggin then right into Finkle Street and return to the town centre.

Hartforth & Jagger Lane

Length of walk: 4 miles
Start: Gilling West
Terrain: Mostly field walking. Plenty of roadside car parking opposite the Post Office and a bus service No 29 from Richmond

Walk past St. Agatha's church, cross Gilling Bridge and continue for 20 yards before swinging left to pass through a wicket gate. Walk past a huge sycamore and locate a stile leading into a field (corn, July 1998). Where the field path divides, follow the left fork across the middle of the field, to a stile.

Maintaining the same line a succession of stiles are crossed, to arrive at the peaceful hamlet of Hartforth. Before leaving the last field notice the barn on the right. This looks as though it was formerly a chapel.

Beyond Home Farm turn left along a lane, noticing Hartforth Hall (a hotel), built in 1720 by William Cradock of Gilling, on your right. Cross Hartforth Beck, then continue straight ahead to a waymarker and proceed to a stile at the opposite end of the field.

The course being followed is known as Jagger Lane: an ancient route used by pack

11

ponies transporting lead from the Swaledale mines to Stockton and Darlington.

Cross a stile then a footbridge, and continue uphill walking close to a depression between avenues of mature trees. Note the pond on your left. Pass through a gate to enter Lambert Wood. Beyond the wood, walk along the edges of two adjoining fields never deviating from the line followed from Hartforth.

Cross a cattle grid, then pass a metal roofed barn, keeping in close contact with the wall to the left. Ten yards beyond the wall angle, close to a large ash tree, swing left through a gate to walk alongside the wall following a pleasant green path towards a plantation known as The Ashes, Gilling West bound.

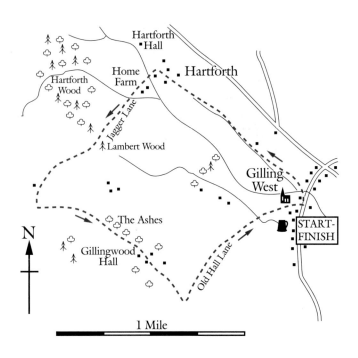

This section offers some superb views as well as the busy A66 road. Later on, Bilsdale Mast will be observed directly ahead on the skyline.

Ignore the gate leading into the plantation. Keep following the wall to pass through Gillingwood Hall Farm, a tidy, well-tended establishment. Leave by the access road, Old Hall Lane, Gilling West will be in sight as the junction is approached.

Cross over the main road and a stile then locate another stile beneath an archway in the hedge. From this point head towards the church, seeking a stile in the wall. Pass through the graveyard, noting the amusing inscription on a tombstone just beyond the church doorway. Sadly you're left to speculate what the final line should be!

Around the fields to Aske Hall

Length of walk: 6 miles
Start: Gilling West
Terrain: Easy. Lots of field walking
Plenty of roadside parking opposite the Post Office
and a bus service No 29 from Richmond

Leave the village along Millgate situated close to the Post Office. Pass a redundant Wesleyan chapel and continue to the end of the road to enter the children's play area and the fields beyond.

Pass to the left side of the sewerage works, treading a path which skirts the edge of the fields, alongside a beck. Cross Crayfish Beck by the footbridge then continue the previous course to arrive at a gate. This leads onto a farm road — turn right towards Gascoigne Farm.

Cross the cattle grid and continue past the buildings then swing right to arrive at a gate. Pass through, then follow the track uphill to another gate; wonderful views unfurl all the time. Beyond the gate curve left downhill to another gate but don't pass through. Instead, stop, turn around and head diagonally left across the open field seeking a stile and a waymark, hidden in the top corner of the field near the trees (no waymarks). There's a path on the map but not on the ground!

From the hidden stile walk in a straight line, passing Olliver Farm, to emerge onto the main road close to Aske Bridge. Because there's no access to Aske Hall at this location, you must turn right and follow the busy road until the lodge and signboard "to Zetland Woodcrafts" are encountered.

Enter Aske Hall grounds walking along the driveway beyond the "woodcrafts" turning, then follow the waymarks to arrive at the front of the

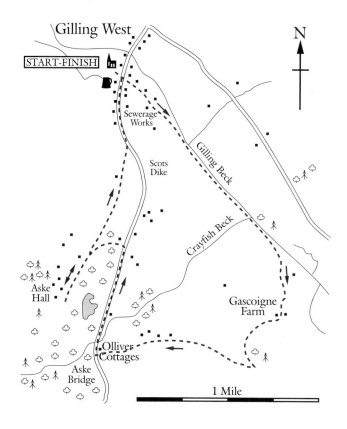

house. Pause a while to appreciate the architectural splendour of the building and the open aspects of the grounds and lake.

The Aske Hall estate has been in the possession of the Dundas family (Lord Zetland) since 1760. The original buildings are much older, and were home to the Aske family for 500 years before the reign of Henry VIII!

When ready, about turn and retrace your footsteps towards the woodcraft centre junction, seeking a bright yellow waymark and a stile directly ahead.

From the stile proceed straight ahead (with mature trees on your right). Pass through a gate, then follow a clear track downhill with the red roofs of Gilling West in sight.

Cross a stile alongside a white gate and descend to the road, passing a piggery on the way. At the road turn left to Gilling West.

Three villages

Length of walk:4¹/₂ miles
Start:Ravensworth
Terrain:Field walking
Careful navigation required
Bus service No 79 United Services, from Richmond

An outing revealing three less-known villages of the Richmond area, Ravensworth, Dalton and Gayles. Each is a delightful location, exuding local pride in well-maintained properties and colourful gardens. All have a public house as well!

Begin this "navigational adventure" by facing the Bay Horse at Ravensworth. Swing right and take the road out of the village. Just beyond Mill Farm pass through a green gate on the left (signpost) and a second gate to walk a straight line alongside a beck, passing through another wide gate soon after.

Maintain the same direction, along the edge of several fields, crossing a stile along the way, until confronted by a wall. At this point veer left along the field boundary to arrive at a waymarked gate (the right of way crosses the field diagonally).

Pass through the gate, proceeding between a large tree and a mound, then continue across the pasture towards a waymarked gate. With Low Fields farm on your left, walk in a straight line towards a fence angle (ignore the diversion information). Don't pass through the newly installed gate at the angle.

Continue in the same direction as before walking along the field edge, with the hedge on the left. Reaching the corner of the field swing right, then locate a stile on the left after three or four paces. Cross this, heading towards a yellow waymarker with Dalton in sight.

Cross the field to pass through a farmyard — waymarker on barn. At the road turn right, cross the bridge (YNR is the abbreviation for Yorkshire North Riding) and turn left through the stile. Cross the field seeking the exit point to the right of a large house and enter the picturesque village of Dalton.

Tread the road for a few paces, turning left near the telephone box to pass St James's church. Continue uphill seeking a footpath sign on the left and pass through the gate. This is the access track to Dalton Mill — watch out for the geese!

Leave the track on the right (where it bends left) and follow the steps down to a stile to enter Throstle Gill, a sylvan wonderland of immense beauty. The route is well waymarked and generally keeps close to the beck.

Emerging from the woodland into a paddock, cross the footbridge then walk uphill between a large tree and some gorse bushes. A faint path curves slightly left for 200 yards to a gate (waymark). Follow the boundary to another gate, then head diagonally across the field to a stile.

Head across the field making towards some houses in the distance, seeking a waymarked footbridge situated near a solitary tree. Turn left to follow the boundary beyond the angle and through another gate, seeking a narrow exit stile close to some trees. At the road turn right to pass through the village of Gayles.

Beyond the last buildings locate a footpath sign on the left and hop over the gate. Cross the field diagonally to another gate (wet area) turning right.

Follow the field edge, beyond the angle, to a gate at the bottom of the field and swing right. Continue with the hedge on the right, through a succession of gates, seeking a stile resting in a field corner. Cross this, then proceed with the hedge to your left to a stile alongside a holly bush. This leads onto a metalled road — Flatts Bank. Turn left to Ravensworth, passing the remains of the castle.

* An alternative route fom Gayles would be to continue along the road, turning left into Flatts Bank.

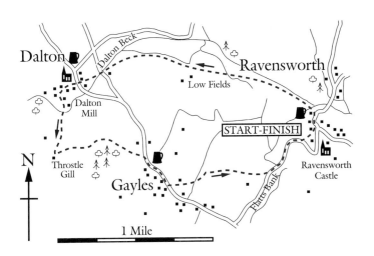

Willance's Leap & the Old Richmond Racecourse

Length of walk: 4½ miles
Start: Twin masts. B6270 Richmond-Marske road
Terrain: Easy going
Navigation: Care needed between Racecourse and Coalsgarth Gate
Ample roadside parking in the vicinity of the twin masts

Make for the footpath sign closest to the masts and cross the stile to follow a well-trodden path to Willance's Leap. The site is so named after Robert Willance, who rode his horse over the edge and survived! The horse died!! The year was 1606.

Having come through the gate, turn left to walk high above the River Swale in the direction of Richmond. Eventually the route departs from the cliff edge to enter a field, maintaining the previous line. Skirt to the topside of some gorse bushes, and descend to a stile near High Leases farm (a modern development). Cross the stile, turning left to pass through a gate, and continue straight along the lane.

Reaching a dwelling on the left (formerly Whitcliffe Farm) swing left into a lane. At the top of the lane pass through a gateway, then continue straight ahead following a clear path running between some tussocky grass. Pass through another gate, before entering a narrow enclosed lane via a red gate.

At the road turn right, (then left near a house at a bridleway sign for a shortened route to Coalsgarth Gate), and continue to the old racecourse situated on the left just beyond Gingerfield Lodge. Walking in a straight line, pass to the left side of the ruined grandstand (noting that the last running of the Richmond Gold Cup was in 1891) then descend to a narrow gap stile alongside a tree, to leave the racecourse.

From the stile veer left for a few paces to another stile near the wall angle, then swing left and accompany the boundary wall and fence until it passes a plantation and descends to a gate. Pass through the gate, veering right after a few paces. Pass a section of wall, and continue straight ahead through another gate.

Follow the same line curving slightly right to pass through an open gateway. Immediately after this turn right to pass through another gate. Having made this crucial manoeuvre, turn left to resume the previous line walking along a well defined path, seeking a stile situated at the far end of the enclosure on the left. (This leads to Coalsgarth Gate, which was offered as the shorter option.)

Entering the lane turn right, pass through the wide gate and head uphill to another gate. Don't pass through this gate; instead veer left to follow a clear path which wriggles through the plantation leading back to the masts.

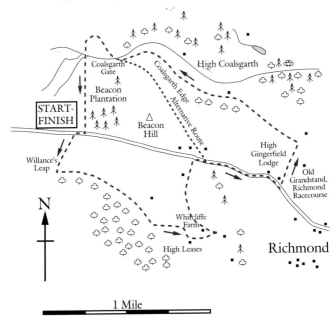

Skelton Moor

Length of walk: 6 miles
Start: Marske Bridge
Terrain: Woodland. Moorland
(not to be considered in misty conditions)

Marske, pronounced Mask, was formerly the home of the Hutton family. They lived at Marske Hall and are remembered in the church, which was rebuilt in the 18th century. A tall obelisk standing on a hill overlooking the village is a monument to Timothy Hutton.

Marske Bridge dates from the 15th century, although nearby Pillimire Bridge is much older. It was built originally for the Nuns of Marrick Priory, although the present construction dates from the late 18th century. The old overshot wheel nearby generated electricity for Skelton Hall. These historical features will be seen towards the end of the walk.

From Marske Bridge pass through the facing stile, head up the field passing to the left of the houses and aiming for a stile at the top of the field. Turn left following a wide track into the woods (ignore the Private Woodland signs) carpeted in bluebells and wild garlic in season. Where the path divides, take the left fork.

Beyond the woods with the white limestone of Clint Scar clearly visible, join a concrete access road (Orgate Farm) and swing left, downhill. Cross the beck and continue straight ahead to walk along the access road to Telfit Farm. Immediately before the farm, swing left to begin the ascent to Skelton Moor. The path curves upwards to a gate, then continues, with the wall to the right, to another gate and onto the moor.

Within a few paces the path crosses another track and offers a choice of routes. Those wanting a shortened version should swing left to follow the newly encountered path, saving about 1¼ miles. If you're sticking with the moorland crossing, keep straight ahead, rising along a green swathe to cross the heather clad moorland. A wonderful experience in late summer when the deep purple heather is in bloom.

The path eventually arrives at a gate (beyond which you'll see Green Lane Farm). Don't use the gate — instead complete a hairpin left turn and follow a narrow green path that runs between the heather and the wall to your right. As you head back towards Marske the dark outline of the Hambleton Hills will be visible ahead.

Follow this route to reach a facing gate (the short route merges hereabouts) and continue straight on. Another good viewpoint! Keen eyes will detect Richmond Castle. Pass through another gate, entering an enclosed lane, and descend to the road. Turn right.

Beyond a barn with a tin roof, on the left, go through a stile to cross the field, passing to the right of a tall tree. Cross a stile near a telegraph pole, maintaining the same line, to arrive at Pillimire Bridge and the waterwheel. Cross the bridge and turn right, following Marske Beck to Marske Bridge.

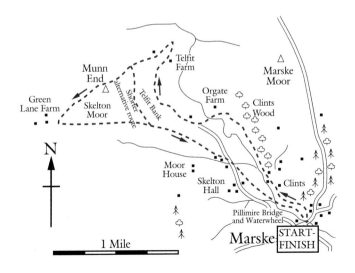

Wanderings around Reeth

Length of walk: 4½ miles
Start: Reeth (King's Arms)
Terrain: Fields, riverside, green lane. Short uphill road section

Any book containing walks around Richmond must include a visit to Reeth. Formerly a lead-mining centre with a population of several thousands, the village has become a tourist centre housing a local community of a few hundred residents.

This outing visits two neighbouring settlements: Grinton (taking time to visit St. Andrew's church) and High Fremington. There's plenty of parking in Reeth.

Set out from the cobbled area in front of the King's Arms, pass Barclays Bank and enter a narrow lane — signposted "to the river". At the lane end turn left, then right to pass the doctor's surgery, before descending to a gate.

Veer right across the fields, cross the suspension bridge and turn left. Walk alongside the river, noting the stepped field ridges (Anglo Saxon cultivation systems) and Reeth School across the river to the left. Maintain the same line across a field to enter an enclosed lane. Eventually the river reappears, and the lane merges with a road — turn left.

Fifty yards beyond a white painted house, pass through a narrow stile on the left and continue between the river and the churchyard to emerge at a main road in Grinton. Turn left, cross Grinton Bridge and swing right to rejoin the riverside path. Note the "old" and "new" arches — a result of bridge-widening a century ago.

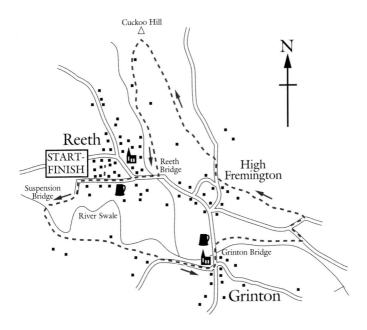

Cross three stiles before leaving the riverside, to rise to another stile and onto a road. Turn left, follow the road to a junction and turn right to follow the road uphill for 200 yards seeking a stile on the left — signpost "Fremington".

Cross the field to a narrow stile, maintaining the same course through a succession of stiles to arrive at a narrow tarred lane. Turn right and follow the lane until a signpost to Arkengarthdale is reached on the left. At this juncture leave the hard surface and begin a ¹/₂ mile stroll along a green lane which offers superb views of Reeth.

The lane terminates at a gate, but continue on to a stile 100 yards beyond and swing left. Pass to the right of a large barn to pass through two stiles in quick succession. Beyond these swing left towards a stile beneath a large tree and on through two fields to emerge at Reeth Bridge. Cross the bridge and return into the village.

Grinton Lead Mines

Length of walk: 3½ miles
Start: Grinton Youth Hostel
Terrain: High ground around Sharrow Hill

Grinton Lodge was built as a shooting lodge in the early part of the 19th century. Its castellated walls and tower look somewhat incongruous in the moorland setting high above Grinton village. For the past 50 years the lodge has served as a youth hostel.

Park alongside the road close to the youth hostel, then set off uphill walking on the closely cropped roadside grass. Cross a road bridge and after 10 yards turn right to follow a clear path upwards to Grinton Smelt Mill, a well-preserved site formerly associated with the lead mining industry.

The first building encountered used to be a peat store, with the smelting

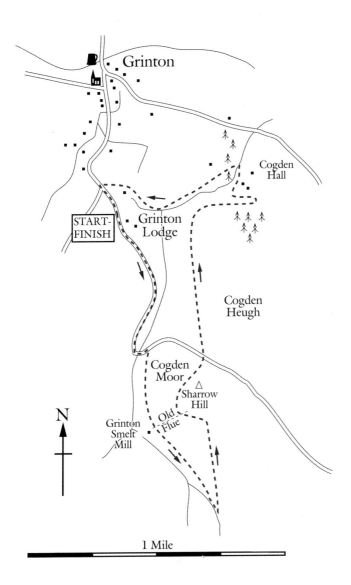

Grinton

Cogden
Hall

START-
FINISH

Grinton
Lodge

Cogden
Heugh

Cogden
Moor

Sharrow
Hill

N

Grinton
Smelt
Mill

Old
Flue

1 Mile

furnaces incorporated in the building further right. The highly toxic lead fumes were dispelled through the flue which originally adjoined the smelting building, and still travels up the hillside to the top of Sharrow Hill (Sharrow means boundary, and the eastern parish boundary of Grinton passes close to the hill top).

Keep left of the buildings following a green track upwards towards the spoil tips. Veer left at a fork, maintaining an uphill course and seeking a well-concealed hairpin left turn.

This important manoeuvre is undertaken after the track curves left, and a pointed cairn appears on the distant skyline. Look for a green swathe running between the heather. This deteriorates within a few yards continuing across the moorland as a faint path to arrive at the top end of the flue, near Sharrow Hill.

From the flue top (formerly there was a chimney here) descend a few yards, then veer right to walk beneath the rocky outcrops of Sharrow Hill, following a green track to the road. Cross the road, go through the gate and commence a wonderful descent to Cogden Hall Farm, a stylish Georgian farmhouse built in 1740.

Pass between the outbuildings, turn left along the access road, seeking a stile on the left. Follow a clear path, uphill, between a woodland setting to arrive at another stile.

As you walk above Cogden Beck, Grinton Lodge comes into view. Keep walking, with a wall on the right, to arrive at a gate (ignore a gated stile along the way). Pass through the gate, swing right to hop over a private water supply, proceeding, with the wall to your right, to reach the road. Turn left to Grinton Lodge.

Marrick &
the Nuns' Causey

Length of walk: 3 miles
Start: Marrick village
Terrain: Uphill from Marrick Priory to village

Marrick is another Swaledale village formerly associated with lead mining. The village houses several large farms and a sprinkling of residents. Population numbers swell during summer months when the holiday cottages are inhabited. The Coast to Coast walk passes through this sleepy place.

Set off from the seat on the small triangular green, heading out of the village along the road. After 400 yards locate a stile on the left (footpath signpost). Make towards a wooden gate situated at the top of the field, but a few steps before reaching it pass through a stile on the right. Now turn left, walking, alongside the wall, through several intervening gates, to arrive at a road — turn left. This is the ancient Richmond-Reeth road. A mountain pass of its day!

As the road tilts downwards, note the well-preserved limekiln on the right. Also evident are wonderful views of the Swale valley, with Grinton conspicuous too.

The road twists and turns for half a mile until a signpost is located on the left. At that point leave the road; pass through the stile and head downhill, through a hawthorn copse, never straying far from the boundary on the left.

Below the copse swing left towards the fence and cross a stile alongside a gate. From this point cross the meadows by a succession of stiles to arrive on an access road at Marrick Abbey Farm. The scant remains of Marrick Priory, which formerly housed Nuns of the Benedictine Order, are close by.

Turn left along the road and walk beyond the farm and the outdoor activities centre, veering left through a wide gate (Coast to Coast sign). Ascend a green path noting the seat marking a site on the Turner Location Trail. (J.M.W. Turner, R.A., the famous landscape artist, painted many scenes in the area, including Marrick Priory.)

Pass through the gate to commence the uphill section known as the Nuns' Causey. At the top of the enclosed incline look for the ruins of Ellerton Priory (Nuns of the Cistercian Order), nestling in the valley far below.

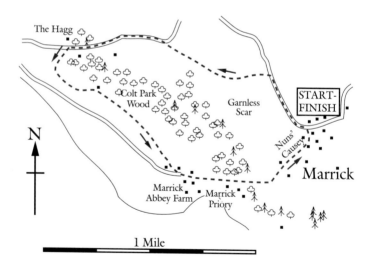

After emerging in a field, follow the wall on the right towards the houses, passing through three metal gates, in quick succession, to arrive at the former Wesleyan chapel (1878). Continue to the first junction turning left at The Old Blacksmith's shop to return to the seat and the tiny green.